MIGHTY JACKIE
THE STRIKE-OUT QUEEN

Marissa Moss
Illustrated by C. F. Payne

A PAULA WISEMAN BOOK

SIMON & SCHUSTER BOOKS FOR YOUNG READERS
NEW YORK LONDON TORONTO SYDNEY SINGAPORE

It was April 2, 1931, and something amazing was about to happen. In Chattanooga, Tennessee, two teams were about to play an exhibition game of baseball.

One was the New York Yankees, a legendary team with famous players—Babe Ruth, Lou Gehrig, and Tony Lazzeri.

The other was the Chattanooga Lookouts, a small team, a nothing team, except for the pitcher, Jackie Mitchell.

Jackie was young, only seventeen years old, but that's not what made people sit up and take notice. Jackie was a girl, and everyone knew that girls didn't play major-league baseball.

The *New York Daily News* sneered that she would swing "a mean lipstick" instead of a bat. A reporter wrote that you might as well have "a trained seal behind the plate" as have a woman standing there. But Jackie was no trained seal. She was a pitcher, a mighty good one. The question was, was she good enough to play against the New York Yankees?

As long as she could remember, Jackie had played ball
with her father. She knew girls weren't supposed to.
All the kids at school, all the boys in her neighborhood told
her that. When one boy yelled at another one, "You throw
like a girl!" it was an insult—everyone knew girls couldn't
throw. Or that's what they thought.

Day after day, in the neighborhood sandlot, Jackie's father told her differently. He said she could throw balls, and she did. She ran bases, she swung the bat. By the time she was eight years old, Dazzy Vance, the star pitcher for the Brooklyn Dodgers, had taught her how to pitch. A real pitcher talking to a little girl was all Jackie needed to start dreaming of playing in the World Series. Her father saw her talent and so did Dazzy. He told her she could be good at whatever she wanted, as long as she worked at it. And Jackie worked at baseball. She worked hard.

She practiced pitching till it was too cold and dark to stay outside. She threw balls until her shoulder ached and her fingers were callused. She pitched until her eyes blurred over and she couldn't see where she was throwing. But it didn't matter, her arm knew.

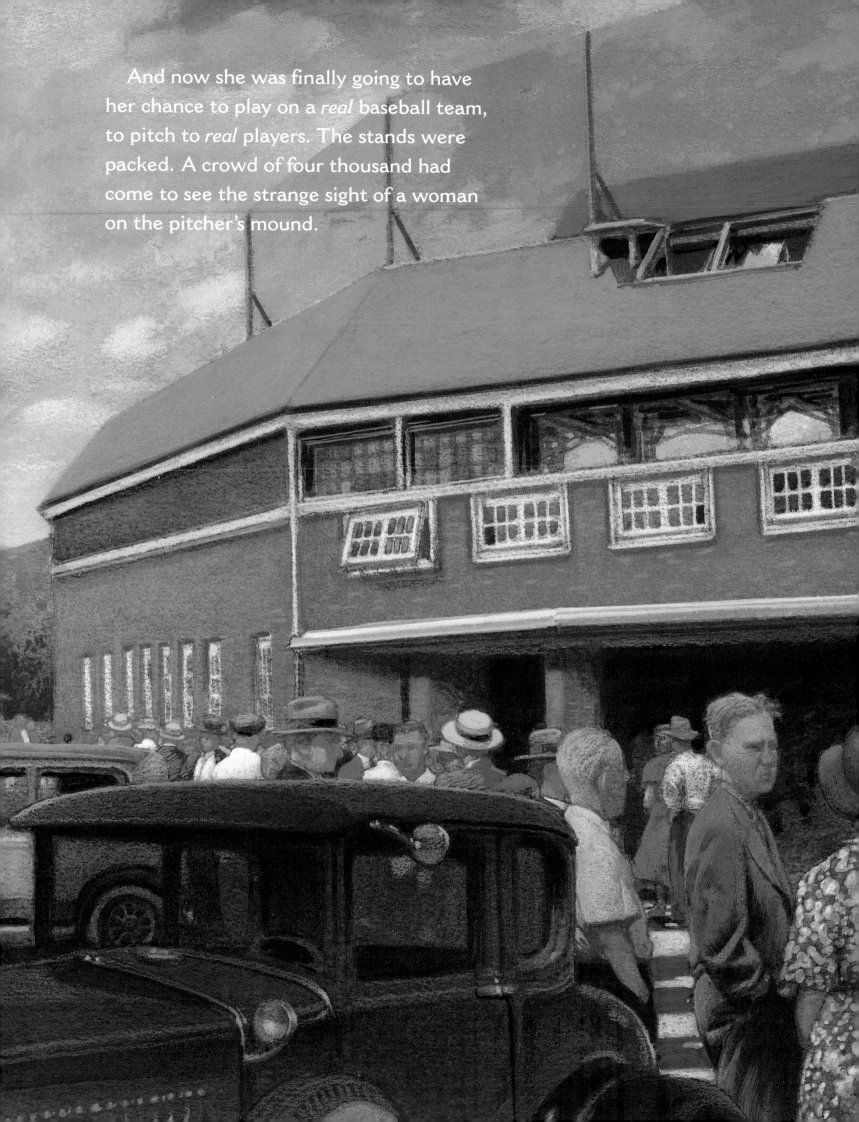

And now she was finally going to have her chance to play on a *real* baseball team, to pitch to *real* players. The stands were packed. A crowd of four thousand had come to see the strange sight of a woman on the pitcher's mound.

She stood tall on the field and looked back at the crowd in the bleachers. They were waiting for her to make a mistake, and she knew it. They were waiting for her to prove that baseball was a man's game, not *her* game.

"It *is* my game," she muttered to herself and bit her lip. The Yankees were up, top of the first, and the batter was walking up to the plate. Jackie was ready for him, the ball tight in her left hand.

Except the batter was Babe Ruth—Babe Ruth, the "Home Run King," a big mountain of a man—and Babe didn't like the idea of a woman pitcher at all. He thought women were "too delicate" for baseball. "They'll never make good," he said. "It would kill them to play ball every day." He walked to the plate and tipped his cap at Jackie. But if she thought he was going to go easy on her, she could forget it! He gripped the bat and got ready to slam the ball out of the ballpark.

Jackie held that ball like it was part of her arm, and when she threw it, she knew exactly where it would go. Right over the plate, right where the Babe wasn't expecting it, right where he watched it speed by and *thwunk* into the catcher's mitt.

"STRRRRIKE ONE!"

Babe Ruth gaped—he couldn't believe it! The crowd roared. Jackie tried to block them out, to see only the ball, to feel only the ball. But Babe Ruth was facing her down now, determined not to let a girl make a fool out of him. She flinched right before the next pitch, and the umpire called a ball.

"Hmmmph," the Babe snorted.

"You can do it!" Jackie told herself. "Girls can throw—show them!"

But the next pitch was another ball.

Now the crowd was hooting and jeering. The Babe was snickering with them.

Jackie closed her eyes. She felt her fingers tingling around the ball, she felt its heft in her palm, she felt the force of her shoulder muscles as she wound up for the pitch. She remembered what her father had told her: "Go out there and pitch just like you pitch to anybody else."

"STRRRRIKE TWO!"

Now the Babe was mad.

This was serious. The Babe was striking out,
and the pitcher was a girl!

Jackie wasn't mad, but she wasn't scared either. She was pitching, really pitching, and it felt like something was happening the way it had always been meant to. She knew the batter would expect the same pitch, close and high, even if the batter was Babe Ruth. So this time she threw the ball straight down the middle with all the speed she could put on it.

"STRRRRIKE THREE!"

Babe Ruth glared at the umpire and threw the bat down in disgust. He told reporters that that would be the last time he'd bat against a woman! The crowd was stunned. A girl had struck out the "Sultan of Swat"! It couldn't be! It was a mistake, a fluke! What would the papers say tomorrow? But wait, here came Lou Gehrig, the "Iron Horse," up to the plate. He'd show her. She couldn't strike him out too.

Lou Gehrig swung with a mighty grunt, but his bat hit nothing but air.

"STRRRRIKE ONE!"

He looked stunned, then dug in his heels and glared at Jackie.

"STRRRRIKE TWO!"

Jackie grinned. She was doing what she'd worked
so hard and long to do, and nothing could stop her.

She pitched the ball the way she knew best, a lefty
pitch with a low dip in it. No one could touch
a ball like that when it was thrown right.

"STRRRRIKE

The crowd, so ready to boo her before, rose with a
roar, clapping and cheering like crazy. Back to back,
Jackie had struck out two of baseball's best batters, Babe
Ruth and Lou Gehrig. She'd proven herself and now the
fans loved her for it.

But Jackie didn't hear them. She was too proud and
too happy. She'd done what she'd always known she
could do. She'd shown the world how a girl could
throw—as hard and as fast and as far as she wanted.

To Myriam and all the students at the American School at Casablanca—M. M.

For Paula—C. F. P.

The author and publisher gratefully acknowledge the assistance of
the National Baseball Hall of Fame Library, Cooperstown, New York, in creating this book.

Author's Note

After Jackie Mitchell's famous game against the Yankees, the baseball commissioner, Kenesaw Mountain Landis, voided her contract with the Chattanooga Lookouts, proclaiming that he was protecting her since baseball was "too strenuous" for a woman. Despite being officially banned from playing in the major and minor leagues, Jackie continued to pitch in the minors, for teams so small and unknown, the baseball commissioner paid no attention to them. For nearly five years she traveled the country, pitching her best, even if the other players weren't of the same caliber as the New York Yankees. She played primarily against men's minor league and semipro teams, but she did have a chance to pitch against the St. Louis Cardinals and struck out Leo Durocher. Realizing that she'd never pitch in the World Series as she once dreamed, and tired of feeling part of a sideshow, Jackie returned to Chattanooga and gave up baseball. But she continues to be known as "The Girl Who Struck Out Babe Ruth."

Bibliography

Berlage, Gai Ingham. *Women in Baseball*. Westport, Conn.: Greenwood Publishing Group, 1994.

Browne, Lois. *Girls of Summer: The Real Story of the All-American Girls Professional Baseball League.* New York: Harper Collins, 1993.

Gregorich, Barbara. *Women at Play: The Story of Women in Baseball.* New York: Harvest Books, 1993.

The Chattanooga News, "Jackie Mitchell Hurls Against Home-Run King," 31 March 1931.
"Famous Players to Play with Invading Club," 2 April 1931. "Lookouts Lose to Yanks 14-4."

New York Daily News, 2 April 1931.

New York Times, 4 April 1931.

SIMON & SCHUSTER BOOKS FOR YOUNG READERS
An imprint of Simon & Schuster Children's Publishing Division • 1230 Avenue of the Americas, New York, New York 10020
Text copyright © 2004 by Marissa Moss • Illustrations copyright © 2004 by C. F. Payne
The photograph on this page is from the National Baseball Hall of Fame Library, Cooperstown, New York.
Reproduction of Jackie Mitchell's signature used by permission of the National Baseball Hall of Fame Library, Cooperstown, New York
All rights reserved, including the right of reproduction in whole or in part in any form.
SIMON & SCHUSTER BOOKS FOR YOUNG READERS is a trademark of Simon & Schuster, Inc.
Book design by Dan Potash
The text for this book is set in Cantoria. The illustrations for this book are rendered in mixed media. Manufactured in China
2 4 6 8 10 9 7 5 3 1
Library of Congress Cataloging-in-Publication Data. Moss, Marissa. Mighty Jackie : the strike-out queen / Marissa Moss ; illustrated by C.F. Payne.— 1st ed.
p. cm. "A Paula Wiseman Book." Summary: In 1931, seventeen-year-old Jackie Mitchell pitches against Babe Ruth and Lou Gehrig in an exhibition game, becoming the first professional female pitcher in baseball history. ISBN 0-689-86329-2 • 1. Mitchell, Jackie, 1914-1987—Juvenile literature. 2. Ruth, Babe, 1895-1948—Juvenile literature. 3. Gehrig, Lou, 1903-1941—Juvenile literature. 4. Women baseball players—United States—Biography—Juvenile literature. [1. Mitchell, Jackie, 1914-1987. 2. Ruth, Babe, 1895-1948. 3. Gehrig, Lou, 1903-1941. 4. Women baseball players. 5. Baseball players. 6. Baseball—History.] I. Payne, C. F., ill. II. Title. GV865.M53 M67 2004 • 796.357'092—dc21 • 2003007382

first edition